Discover the Healthier Way to Cook with Diabetes Cookbook

New Recipe Ideas for You

Evelin Turk

Table of Contents

Cucumber-buttermilk Vichyssoise

Servings: 4

Ingredients:

2 teaspoons extra virgin olive oil

1⁄2 large sweet onion, chopped

2 garlic cloves, minced

2 cups Chicken Stock or low-sodium chicken broth

2 large hothouse (English) cucumbers, peeled, seeded, and chopped

1 large baking potato, peeled and chopped (about 1 1⁄2 cups)

1⁄2 teaspoon kosher salt

Pinch of white pepper

1 cup low-fat buttermilk

Chopped fresh dill sprigs or thinly sliced fresh basil leaves

Directions:

1. Heat a large pot over medium heat. Add the oil and tilt the pan to coat the bottom evenly. Add the onion and cook, stirring often, until softened, 5 minutes. Add the garlic and cook, stirring constantly, until fragrant, 30 seconds. Add the stock, cucumbers, potato, salt, and pepper and bring to a boil over high heat. Reduce the heat to low, cover, and simmer until the vegetables are very tender, 15 to 20 minutes.
2. Place the vegetable mixture in a food processor or blender in batches and process until smooth. Transfer to a large bowl and let cool to room temperature. Stir in the buttermilk, cover, and refrigerate until chilled, at least 2 hours or up to 2 days. Ladle into 4 bowls, sprinkle with the dill, and serve.

Nutrition Info:

25 g carb, 153 cal, 3 g fat, 1 g sat fat, 6 mg chol, 3 g fib, 7 g pro, 284 mg sod • Carb Choices: 1 1⁄2; Exchanges: 1 starch, 1⁄2 carb, 1⁄2 fat

Grilled Chile-rubbed Tuna with Avocado-tomato Salsa

Servings: 4

Ingredients:

FISH

2 teaspoons grated lime zest

1 tablespoon lime juice

1 1⁄2 teaspoons ancho chile powder

21⁄2 teaspoons extra virgin olive oil, divided

4 (5-ounce) tuna steaks

1⁄4 teaspoon kosher salt

SALSA

1 avocado, pitted, peeled, and chopped

1 large tomato, chopped

2 tablespoons minced red onion

1 jalapeño, seeded and minced

1⁄4 cup chopped fresh cilantro

2 tablespoons lime juice

1⁄4 teaspoon kosher salt

Lime wedges

Directions:

1. Preheat the grill to medium-high heat.
2. To make the fish, stir together the lime zest, lime juice, chile powder, and 2 teaspoons of the oil in a shallow dish. Add the tuna and turn to coat. Cover and refrigerate 30 minutes.
3. To make the salsa, combine all the ingredients except the lime wedges in a small bowl.
4. Remove the tuna from the marinade and discard the marinade. Sprinkle the tuna with the salt. Brush the grill rack with the remaining 1⁄2 teaspoon oil. Place the tuna on the grill, and grill 2 minutes on each side for medium-rare, or to the desired degree of doneness. Divide the tuna and salsa evenly among 4 plates and serve at once with the lime wedges.

Nutrition Info:

8 g carb, 269 cal, 12 g fat, 2 g sat fat, 62 mg chol, 4 g fib, 33 g pro, 197 mg sod • Carb Choices: 1⁄2; Exchanges: 1 veg, 4 lean protein, 2 fat

Tomato, Black Bean, And Corn Salsa

Servings: 2 Cups

Ingredients:

1 cup canned no-salt-added black beans, rinsed and drained

1 small ear corn, kernels cut from the cob, or 1⁄2 cup frozen corn kernels, thawed

1 medium tomato, chopped

1 jalapeño, seeded and minced

1⁄4 cup diced green bell pepper

2 tablespoons chopped fresh cilantro

2 tablespoons lime juice

2 teaspoons canola oil

1⁄2 teaspoon kosher salt

Directions:

1. Combine all the ingredients in a medium bowl and stir to mix well. Serve at room temperature within 2 hours.

Nutrition Info:

8 g carb, 49 cal, 1 g fat, 0 g sat fat, 0 mg chol, 2 g fib, 2 g pro, 76 mg sod • Carb Choices: 1⁄2; Exchanges: 1⁄2 starch

Cobb Salad

Servings: 4

Ingredients:

2 strips center-cut bacon

4 cups chopped romaine lettuce

2 cups chopped Bibb lettuce

6 ounces diced cooked chicken breast (about 1 cup)

1 medium tomato, chopped

1 hard-boiled egg, chopped

1/2 avocado, pitted, peeled, and chopped

3 tablespoons crumbled blue cheese

3 tablespoons Basic Vinaigrette

Directions:

1. Cook the bacon in a large skillet over medium-high heat until crisp. Drain on paper towels and coarsely chop.
2. Combine the romaine and Bibb lettuces in a large serving bowl. Arrange the bacon, chicken, tomato, egg, avocado, and blue cheese decoratively over the lettuce.
3. Drizzle with the vinaigrette and toss to coat. Serve at once.

Nutrition Info:

6 g carb, 234 cal, 15 g fat, 4 g sat fat, 97 mg chol, 3 g fib, 19 g pro, 259 mg sod • Carb Choices: 1⁄2; Exchanges: 1 veg, 21⁄2 lean protein, 2 fat

Sesame-roasted Tofu And Vegetables with Asian Pesto

Servings: 4

Ingredients:

2 teaspoons canola oil

1 (1-pound) package firm reduced-fat tofu

3 teaspoons Asian sesame oil, divided

6 thin scallions, white and light green parts cut into 2-inch pieces

1 large red bell pepper, thinly sliced

1⁄2 teaspoon kosher salt

4 tablespoons Asian Pesto

Directions:

1. Preheat the oven to 425°F. Brush a large rimmed baking sheet with the canola oil.
2. Cut the tofu in half lengthwise, then cut each piece in half crosswise. Pat the tofu dry with paper towels.
3. Brush the tofu with 1 teaspoon of the sesame oil and arrange in a single layer on one end of the prepared baking sheet. Place the scallions and bell pepper on the other end of the baking sheet. Drizzle with the remaining 2 teaspoons sesame oil, sprinkle with the salt, and toss to coat. Arrange the vegetables in a single layer. Bake, stirring the vegetables and turning the tofu once, until tender and lightly browned, 30 to 35 minutes.
4. To serve, divide the tofu and vegetables evenly among 4 plates. Top each serving of tofu with 1 tablespoon of the pesto.

Nutrition Info:

10 g carb, 228 cal, 15 g fat, 2 g sat fat, 2 mg chol, 4 g fib, 15 g pro, 301 mg sod • Carb Choices: 1⁄2; Exchanges: 1⁄2 starch, 1 veg, 2 plant- based protein, 2 fat

Cut-out Cookies

Servings: 24

Ingredients:

1 1⁄2 cups unbleached all-purpose flour

1⁄4 teaspoon baking soda

1⁄8 teaspoon salt

4 tablespoons (1⁄2 stick) unsalted butter, softened

1⁄3 cup sugar

1 large egg

1 teaspoon vanilla extract or 1⁄2 teaspoon almond extract

Directions:

1. Combine the flour, baking soda, and salt in a medium bowl and whisk to mix well.
2. Place the butter in a large bowl and beat at medium speed with an electric mixer until fluffy. Gradually beat in the sugar. Beat in the egg and vanilla. Add the flour mixture and beat at low speed just until blended.
3. Divide the dough in half. Place each half between two sheets of parchment paper and roll to a 1⁄4-inch thickness. Place the dough on a baking sheet and refrigerate 1 hour.
4. Preheat the oven to 375°F. Line 2 baking sheets with parchment paper.
5. Cut the dough into the desired shapes using 11⁄2-inch cookie cutters. Transfer the cookies to the prepared baking sheets. Bake until the edges are lightly browned, 8 to 10 minutes. Cool the cookies on the baking sheets for 2 minutes. Transfer to racks to cool completely. The cookies can be stored in an airtight container at room temperature for up to 3 days.

Nutrition Info:

16 g carb, 112 cal, 4 g fat, 3 g sat fat, 28 mg chol, 0 g fib, 2 g pro, 66 mg sod • Carb Choices: 1; Exchanges: 1 carb, 1⁄2 fat

Roasted Turnips with Honey And Toasted Spices

Servings: 4

Ingredients:

1⁄2 teaspoon fennel seeds

1⁄2 teaspoon coriander seeds

6 whole black peppercorns

1 1⁄2 pounds turnips, peeled and cut into 3⁄4-inch pieces

2 teaspoons extra virgin olive oil

3⁄4 teaspoon kosher salt

1 teaspoon honey

Directions:

1. Preheat the oven to 425°F.
2. Place the fennel, coriander, and pepper in a small dry skillet over medium heat and toast, shaking the pan often, until the spices are fragrant, about 3 minutes. Transfer to a small dish and allow to cool. Place the spices in a mortar and crush with a pestle. Alternatively, place the spices in a small resealable plastic bag. Seal the bag, place on a cutting board, and crush using a meat mallet or the back of a large spoon.
3. Place the turnips on a large rimmed baking sheet. Drizzle with the oil and sprinkle with the toasted spices and the salt. Toss to coat. Arrange the turnips in a single layer.
4. Roast, turning the turnips once, until tender and browned, 35 to 40 minutes.
5. Transfer the turnips to a serving bowl, drizzle with the honey, and toss to coat. Serve hot or warm.

Nutrition Info:

10 g carb, 65 cal, 3 g fat, 0 g sat fat, 0 mg chol, 3 g fib, 1 g pro, 302 mg sod • Carb Choices: 1⁄2; Exchanges: 2 veg, 1⁄2 fat

Grilled Italian Turkey Sausage with Peppers And Tomatoes

Servings: 4

Ingredients:

4 plum tomatoes, halved lengthwise

1 large red onion, cut into 8 wedges

1 green bell pepper, cut into 1-inch slices

1 red or yellow bell pepper, cut into 1-inch slices

2 tablespoons plus 21⁄2 teaspoons extra-virgin olive oil, divided

1 pound hot or mild Italian turkey sausage links

2 tablespoons red wine vinegar

1⁄2 teaspoon Dijon mustard

1 garlic clove, crushed through a press

1⁄4 teaspoon kosher salt

1⁄4 teaspoon dried oregano

1⁄4 teaspoon dried basil

1⁄4 teaspoon freshly ground pepper

Directions:

1. Prepare the grill or heat a large grill pan over medium-high heat.
2. Combine the tomatoes, onion, and bell peppers in a large bowl. Drizzle with 2 teaspoons of the oil and toss to coat.
3. Brush the grill rack or grill pan with 1⁄2 teaspoon of the remaining oil. Pierce the sausages several times using the point of a small knife. Place the sausages, onion, and bell peppers on the grill and grill, turning often, until the juices of the sausages run clear and the vegetables are crisp-tender, about 10 minutes. Place the tomatoes on the grill during the last 3 to 4 minutes of cooking time and grill, turning once, just until heated through.
4. Meanwhile, whisk together the remaining 2 tablespoons oil, the vinegar, mustard, garlic, salt, oregano, basil, and ground pepper in a small bowl. To serve, divide the sausages and vegetables among 4 plates and drizzle evenly with the dressing.

Nutrition Info:

10 g carb, 264 cal, 17 g fat, 3 g sat fat, 64 mg chol, 3 g fib, 18 g pro, 587 mg sod • Carb Choices: 1⁄2; Exchanges: 1 veg, 2 lean protein, 1 1⁄2 fat

Grilled Salmon with Yogurt Sauce

Servings: 4

Ingredients:

1⁄2 cup plain low-fat yogurt

2 tablespoons thinly sliced scallions, green tops only

2 teaspoons lemon juice

1⁄2 teaspoon ground cumin, divided

Pinch plus 1⁄2 teaspoon kosher salt

Pinch of ground cayenne

4 (4-ounce) salmon fillets

1⁄8 teaspoon freshly ground pepper

1⁄2 teaspoon canola oil

Directions:

1. Preheat the grill to medium-high heat.
2. Stir together the yogurt, scallions, lemon juice, 1/4 teaspoon of the cumin, the pinch of salt, and the cayenne in a small bowl. Cover and refrigerate until ready to serve.
3. Sprinkle the salmon with the remaining 1/2 teaspoon salt, the remaining 1/4 teaspoon cumin, and the pepper. Brush the grill rack with the oil. Place the salmon on the grill and grill until the fish is opaque in the center, about 3 minutes on each side. Place the salmon on 4 plates. Spoon the sauce evenly over the salmon and serve at once.

Nutrition Info:

3 g carb, 211 cal, 9 g fat, 2 g sat fat, 73 mg chol, 0 g fib, 27 g pro, 237 mg sod • Carb Choices: 0; Exchanges: 4 lean protein

Cranberry-maple Rice Salad

Servings: 83 Cups Water

Ingredients:

1 1/2 cups long-grain brown rice

1 teaspoon kosher salt, divided

1 cup fresh cranberries or unthawed frozen cranberries

2 tablespoons real maple syrup

1/3 cup orange juice

2 tablespoon extra virgin olive oil

1 tablespoon white wine vinegar

2 teaspoons Dijon mustard

2 teaspoons grated orange zest

1/4 teaspoon freshly ground pepper

1/2 cup diced celery

2 scallions, thinly sliced

1/4 cup chopped fresh Italian parsley

1/4 cup walnuts, toasted and chopped

Directions:

1. Combine the water, rice, and 1⁄2 teaspoon of the salt in a medium saucepan and bring to a boil over high heat. Reduce the heat to low, cover, and simmer until the rice is tender, 35 to 40 minutes. Drain and cool.
2. Meanwhile, combine the cranberries and maple syrup in a small saucepan; bring to a boil over medium heat. Cook, stirring often, until most of the berries pop, about 5 minutes. Transfer to a large bowl to cool.
3. Stir the orange juice, oil, vinegar, mustard, orange zest, pepper, and remaining 1⁄2 teaspoon salt into the cranberry mixture.
4. Add the cooked rice, celery, scallions, and parsley and stir to coat. Stir in the walnuts just before serving. Serve the salad at room temperature. The salad tastes best on the day it is made, but it can be refrigerated, covered, for up to 1 day. Let stand at room temperature 30 minutes before serving.

Nutrition Info:

34 g carb, 212 cal, 7 g fat, 1 g sat fat, 0 mg chol, 3 g fib, 4 g pro, 184 mg sod • Carb Choices: 2; Exchanges: 2 starch, 1 1⁄2 fat

Indian-spiced Turkey Cutlets with Sautéed Peaches

Servings: 4

Ingredients:

4 (4-ounce) turkey breast cutlets

3 teaspoons minced fresh ginger, divided

3⁄4 teaspoon ground cumin, divided

3⁄4 teaspoon ground coriander, divided

1⁄2 teaspoon kosher salt

4 teaspoons canola oil, divided

2 large ripe peaches, pitted and sliced

1 scallion, thinly sliced

2 tablespoons chopped fresh cilantro

1 tablespoon lime juice

Lime wedges

Directions:

1. Sprinkle the turkey with 2 teaspoons of the ginger, 1/2 teaspoon of the cumin, 1/2 teaspoon of the coriander, and the salt. Heat a large nonstick skillet over medium heat. Add 2 teaspoons of the oil and tilt the pan to coat the bottom evenly. Add the turkey and cook, turning once, until the juices run clear, about 4 minutes on each side. Transfer to a plate.
2. Increase the heat to medium-high. Add the remaining 2 teaspoons oil to the skillet and tilt the pan to coat the bottom evenly. Add the peaches and scallion, then add the remaining 1 teaspoon ginger, 1/4 teaspoon cumin, and 1/4 teaspoon coriander. Cook, stirring often, until the peaches are warmed through and the scallion is crisp-tender, about 3 minutes. Remove from the heat and stir in the cilantro and lime juice. Divide the turkey among 4 plates. Top evenly with the peach mixture and serve with the lime wedges.

Nutrition Info:

9 g carb, 169 cal, 5 g fat, 0 g sat fat, 34 mg chol, 2 g fib, 22 g pro, 217 mg sod • Carb Choices: 1/2; Exchanges: 1/2 fruit, 3 lean protein, 1 fat

Broccoli Pesto

Servings: 11⁄2 Cups

Ingredients:

5 cups broccoli florets

2 garlic cloves, minced

Pinch of ground cayenne

1 ounce freshly grated Parmesan (about ¼ cup)

1⁄4 cup pine nuts, toasted

1⁄4 cup water

1 teaspoon grated lemon zest

1 tablespoon lemon juice

1 tablespoon extra virgin olive oil

1⁄2 teaspoon kosher salt

Directions:

1. Place the broccoli in a microwave-safe dish and cover with plastic wrap. Microwave on high until the broccoli is tender, yet still bright green, about 5 minutes.
2. Carefully uncover the broccoli and drain in a colander. Let cool slightly and pat dry with paper towels. Transfer the broccoli to a food processor. Add the remaining ingredients and process until the mixture is smooth. Serve at once, or refrigerate, covered, for up to 1 day. Bring to room temperature before serving.

Nutrition Info:

4 g carb, 92 cal, 7 g fat, 1 g sat fat, 3 mg chol, 2 g fib, 4 g pro, 161 mg sod • Carb Choices: 0; Exchanges: 1 veg, 1 1⁄2 fat

Sweet Potato–apple Soup

Servings: 6

Ingredients:

2 teaspoons extra virgin olive oil

1 medium onion, chopped

2 garlic cloves, minced

21⁄2 to 23⁄4 cups Vegetable Stock or low-sodium vegetable broth

1 cup unsweetened apple juice

1 1⁄2 pounds sweet potatoes, peeled and chopped

1⁄2 to 1 teaspoon minced chipotle in adobo sauce

1⁄2 teaspoon kosher salt

2 tablespoons lime juice

Directions:

1. Heat a large saucepan over medium heat. Add the oil and tilt the pan to coat the bottom evenly. Add the onion and cook, stirring often, until softened, 5 minutes. Add the garlic and cook, stirring constantly, until fragrant, 30 seconds. Add 21⁄2 cups of the stock, the apple juice, potatoes, chipotle, and salt and bring to a boil over high heat. Cover, reduce the heat to low, and simmer until the potato is very tender, 15 to 20 minutes.
2. Place the potato mixture in a food processor in batches and process until smooth. Return the soup to the pot reheat over medium heat. Add the remaining 1⁄4 cup stock a few tablespoons at a time, if needed, to reach the desired consistency. Remove from the heat and stir in the lime juice. Ladle the soup into 6 bowls and serve at once. The soup can be refrigerated, covered, for up to 4 days.

Nutrition Info:

23 g carb, 114 cal, 2 g fat, 0 g sat fat, 0 mg chol, 3 g fib, 2 g pro, 247 mg sod • Carb Choices: 11⁄2; Exchanges: 1 starch, 1⁄2 carb

Tomato And Fennel Soup

Servings: 6

Ingredients:

1/2 teaspoon whole fennel seeds

1 large bulb fennel

2 teaspoons extra virgin olive oil

1 large onion, chopped

1 carrot, peeled and chopped

1 stalk celery, chopped

2 garlic cloves, minced

2 (28-ounce) cans no-salt-added whole tomatoes, undrained

1 cup water

1/2 teaspoon kosher salt

1/8 teaspoon freshly ground pepper

Directions:

1. Place the fennel seeds in a small dry skillet over medium heat and toast, shaking the pan often, until the fennel seeds are fragrant, about 3 minutes. Transfer to a small plate and allow to cool. Place the fennel seeds in a mortar and crush with a pestle. Alternatively, place the fennel seeds in a small resealable plastic bag. Seal the bag, place on a cutting board, and crush using a meat mallet or the back of a large spoon.
2. Trim the tough outer stalks from the fennel bulb. Cut the fennel bulb in half vertically and cut away and discard the core. Chop the fennel.
3. Heat a large pot over medium heat. Add the oil and tilt the pan to coat the bottom evenly. Add the fennel bulb, onion, carrot, and celery and cook, stirring often, until softened, 5 minutes. Add the garlic and cook, stirring constantly, until fragrant, 30 seconds.
4. Add the tomatoes with their juice and stir, breaking the tomatoes up with a spoon. Add the water, fennel seeds, salt, and pepper and bring to a boil over high heat. Cover, reduce the heat to low, and simmer until all the vegetables are very tender, 25 to 30 minutes.
5. Place the vegetable mixture in a food processor or blender in batches and process until smooth (add additional water a few tablespoons at a time if necessary to adjust consistency). Return the soup to the pot and reheat over medium heat.
6. Ladle the soup into 6 bowls and serve at once. The soup can be refrigerated, covered, for up to 4 days or frozen for up to 3 months.

Nutrition Info:

16 g carb, 87 cal, 2 g fat, 0 g sat fat, 0 mg chol, 4 g fib, 5 g pro, 329 mg sod • Carb Choices: 1; Exchanges: 3 veg

Chipotle Black Bean Burgers

Servings: 4

Ingredients:

1 (15-ounce) can no-salt-added black beans, rinsed and drained

1⁄3 cup plain dry breadcrumbs

2 tablespoons chopped fresh cilantro

3 tablespoons chopped scallions

1 garlic clove, minced

1 large egg

1⁄2 teaspoon ground cumin

1⁄4 to 1⁄2 teaspoon minced chipotle in adobo sauce

1⁄4 teaspoon kosher salt

2 teaspoons canola oil

4 whole wheat kaiser rolls, split and toasted

1 cup Winter Tomato Salsa or purchased salsa

Lettuce leaves

Directions:

1. Place the beans in a large bowl and mash with a potato masher until chunky. Stir in the breadcrumbs, cilantro, scallion, garlic, egg, cumin, chipotle, and salt. Shape into 4 patties.
2. Heat a large nonstick skillet over medium-high heat. Add the oil and tilt the pan to coat the bottom evenly. Add the burgers and cook, turning once, until lightly browned, 2 to 3 minutes on each side. Serve the burgers in the rolls, topped with the salsa and lettuce.

Nutrition Info:

46 g carb, 289 cal, 6 g fat, 1 g sat fat, 53 mg chol, 10 g fib, 13 g pro, 401 mg sod • Carb Choices: 3; Exchanges: 3 starch, 1 plant-based protein

Grilled Tuna with Wasabi Vinaigrette

Servings: 4

Ingredients:

3 tablespoons reduced-sodium soy sauce

2 tablespoons rice vinegar

1 tablespoon plus 1/2 teaspoon canola oil, divided

2 teaspoons prepared wasabi paste

4 (5-ounce) tuna steaks

Directions:

1. Whisk together the soy sauce, vinegar, 1 tablespoon of the oil, and the wasabi paste in a medium bowl. Place the tuna in a medium shallow dish and drizzle with 1 tablespoon of the soy sauce mixture. Turn the tuna to coat. Cover and refrigerate 30 minutes.
2. Preheat the grill to medium-high heat.
3. Brush the grill rack with the remaining 1⁄2 teaspoon oil. Remove the tuna from the marinade and discard the marinade. Place the tuna on the grill and grill, turning once, 2 minutes on each side for medium rare, or to the desired degree of doneness. Place the tuna on 4 plates, drizzle evenly with the remaining soy sauce mixture, and serve at once.

Nutrition Info:

1 g carb, 191 cal, 5 g fat, 1 g sat fat, 62 mg chol, 0 g fib, 33 g pro, 560 mg sod • Carb Choices: 0; Exchanges: 4 lean protein, 1 fat

Sour Cream Pound Cake

Servings: 16

Ingredients:

1 teaspoon plus 4 tablespoons (1⁄2 stick) unsalted butter, softened, divided

2 cups cake flour plus flour for dusting the pan

2 teaspoons baking powder

1⁄2 teaspoon baking soda

1⁄4 teaspoon salt

1 cup sugar

2 large eggs

1 cup reduced-fat sour cream

1 tablespoon vanilla extract

Directions:

1. Preheat the oven to 350°F. Brush an 81⁄2 x 41⁄2-inch loaf pan with 1 teaspoon of the butter. Dust the pan lightly with flour, shaking the pan to remove the excess.
2. Combine the 2 cups flour, baking powder, baking soda, and salt in a medium bowl and whisk to mix well.
3. Place the remaining 4 tablespoons butter in a large mixing bowl and beat at medium speed with an electric mixer until fluffy. Gradually beat in the sugar. Beat in the eggs one at a time. Add the sour cream and vanilla and beat until smooth. Add the flour mixture and beat at low speed just until smooth.
4. Spoon the batter into the pan and bake until a wooden toothpick inserted in the center of the loaf comes out clean, 50 to 55 minutes.
5. Cool the cake in the pan on a wire rack for 10 minutes. Remove from the pan and cool completely on a wire rack before slicing. The cake can be covered in an airtight container and stored at room temperature for up to 3 days.

Nutrition Info:

25 g carb, 157 cal, 6 g fat, 3 g sat fat, 40 mg chol, 0 g fib, 2 g pro, 141 mg sod • Carb Choices: 11⁄2; Exchanges: 11⁄2 carb, 1 fat

Roasted Eggplant And Spinach Salad with Peanut Dressing

Servings: 4

Ingredients:

1 tablespoon plus 1 teaspoon canola oil, divided

1 medium eggplant (about 11⁄4 pounds), cut into 1⁄2-inch rounds

1⁄4 teaspoon kosher salt

6 cups loosely packed torn fresh spinach

1 recipe Peanut Dressing

2 tablespoons chopped fresh cilantro

Directions:

1. Preheat the oven to 425°F. Brush a large rimmed baking sheet with 1 teaspoon of the oil.
2. Brush the eggplant slices with the remaining 1 tablespoon oil. Sprinkle with the salt. Arrange in a single layer on the baking sheet. Bake, turning once, until tender and well browned, 35 to 40 minutes. Transfer to a platter and let cool to room temperature.
3. Place the spinach in a large bowl, drizzle with 2 tablespoons of the dressing, and toss to coat. Divide the spinach among 4 plates and top evenly with the eggplant. Drizzle the eggplant evenly with the remaining dressing, sprinkle with the cilantro, and serve at once.

Nutrition Info:

13 g carb, 158 cal, 10 g fat, 1 g sat fat, 0 mg chol, 6 g fib, 5 g pro, 351 mg sod • Carb Choices: 1⁄2; Exchanges: 1⁄2 carb, 2 fat

Butternut Squash And Gruyère Gratin

Servings: 8

Ingredients:

5 teaspoons extra virgin olive oil, divided

2 large onions, thinly sliced

3⁄4 teaspoon kosher salt, divided

1 tablespoon chopped fresh rosemary

1⁄4 teaspoon freshly ground pepper

1 large butternut squash (about 3 pounds), peeled, seeded, and cut into 1⁄4-inch slices

3 ounces shredded Gruyère (about 3⁄4 cup), divided

3⁄4 cup fresh whole wheat breadcrumbs

Directions:

1. Heat a large nonstick skillet over medium heat. Add 2 teaspoons of the oil and tilt the pan to coat the bottom evenly. Add the onions and 1⁄4 teaspoon of the salt and cook, stirring occasionally, until very soft and browned, about 25 minutes. Stir in the rosemary and pepper and set aside.
2. Preheat the oven to 350°F. Brush a shallow 3-quart baking dish with 1 teaspoon of the remaining oil. Place one-third of the squash slices in the dish and sprinkle with 1⁄4 teaspoon of the remaining salt. Top the squash with half of the onion mixture. Top the onions with half of the Gruyère. Top the Gruyère with one-third of the squash slices and sprinkle with the remaining 1⁄4 teaspoon salt. Spread the remaining onions over the squash. Sprinkle with the remaining half of the Gruyère. Top with the remaining one-third of the squash slices.
3. Cover and bake 30 minutes. Uncover and bake 20 more minutes. Stir together the breadcrumbs and the remaining 2 teaspoons oil. Sprinkle over the gratin and bake until the crumbs are browned, 10 minutes longer. Let stand 5 minutes before serving.

Nutrition Info:

21 g carb, 150 cal, 6 g fat, 2 g sat fat, 12 mg chol, 3 g fib, 5 g pro, 176 mg sod • Carb Choices: 1 1⁄2; Exchanges: 1 1⁄2 starch, 1⁄2 high-fat protein

Bacon-basil Mushrooms

Servings: 4

Ingredients:

2 strips center-cut bacon

1 small red onion, cut in half and sliced

2 garlic cloves, minced

1 1⁄2 pounds cremini mushrooms, sliced

1⁄4 teaspoon kosher salt

1⁄4 teaspoon freshly ground pepper

3 tablespoons chopped fresh basil

Directions:

1. Cook the bacon in a large skillet over medium-high heat until crisp. Drain on paper towels and chop. Pour off and discard all but 2 teaspoons of the drippings.
2. Add the onion to the bacon drippings and cook, stirring often, until softened, about 5 minutes. Add the garlic and cook, stirring constantly, until fragrant, 30 seconds. Add the mushrooms and cook, stirring often, until the mushrooms are tender and most of the liquid has evaporated, about 8 minutes. Remove from the heat and stir in the bacon and the basil. Spoon the mushrooms into a serving dish and serve hot or warm.

Nutrition Info:

9 g carb, 88 cal, 3 g fat, 1 g sat fat, 5 mg chol, 1 g fib, 5 g pro, 148 mg sod • Carb Choices: 1⁄2; Exchanges: 1 veg, 1⁄2 fat

Herb Water

Servings: 8

Ingredients:

8 cups cold water, divided

1/4 cup loosely packed fresh basil, dill, mint, or cilantro leaves or 2 tablespoons fresh tarragon leaves or a combination

8 thin lemon slices

Directions:

1. Place 1 cup of the water and the herb of your choice in a blender and process until smooth.
2. Set a fine wire mesh strainer over a 2-quart pitcher. Pour the herb mixture through the strainer. Discard the solids. Add the remaining 7 cups water to the pitcher and refrigerate until chilled, at least 2 hours and up to 2 days.

Nutrition Info:

0 g carb, 0 cal, 0 g fat, 0 g sat fat, 0 mg chol, 0 g fib, 0 g pro, 10 mg sod • Carb Choices: 0

Vanilla Cream Pie

Servings: 12

Ingredients:

1 recipe Pastry Crust

2 cups 1% low-fat milk

1 large egg

1⁄2 cup sugar

3 tablespoons cornstarch

Pinch of salt

2 teaspoons vanilla extract

Directions:

1. Preheat the oven to 400°F.
2. Place the pastry dough between two sheets of wax paper. Roll the dough into a 12-inch circle. Remove the top layer of wax paper and place the dough, with the wax paper facing up, into a 9-inch glass pie plate. Starting from the edge of the dough, gently remove the wax paper. Fold the overhanging dough under and crimp the edge decoratively. Prick the bottom of the crust all over with a fork. Line the crust with parchment paper and fill with pie weights or dried beans. Bake 20 minutes. Remove the parchment and weights and bake until the crust is lightly browned, 5 to 8 minutes. Cool completely on a wire rack.
3. Meanwhile, to make the filling, combine the milk, egg, sugar, cornstarch, and salt in a medium saucepan. Cook over medium heat, whisking constantly, until the mixture comes to a boil and thickens, about 8 minutes. Stir in the vanilla.
4. Spoon the hot filling into the crust. Place a sheet of wax paper directly on the filling and refrigerate 4 hours or until firm. The pie is best on the day it is made.

Nutrition Info:

23 g carb, 147 cal, 5 g fat, 3 g sat fat, 30 mg chol, 1 g fib, 3 g pro, 85 mg sod • Carb Choices: 1½; Exchanges: 1½ carb, 1 fat

Asian Barbecued Chicken

Servings: 4

Ingredients:

2 tablespoons light brown sugar

2 tablespoons reduced-sodium soy sauce

1 tablespoon rice vinegar

2 1/2 teaspoons canola oil, divided

2 garlic cloves, minced

1 teaspoon grated fresh ginger

1 teaspoon five-spice powder

1/2 teaspoon Asian sesame oil

4 (4-ounce) boneless skinless chicken breasts

Lime wedges

Directions:

1. Combine the sugar, soy sauce, vinegar, 2 teaspoons of the canola oil, the garlic, ginger, five-spice powder, and sesame oil in a large resealable plastic bag. Add the chicken, turn to coat, and refrigerate 2 to 4 hours.
2. Preheat the grill to medium-high heat.
3. Remove the chicken from the marinade and discard the marinade. Pat the chicken dry with paper towels.
4. Brush the grill rack with the remaining 1⁄2 teaspoon canola oil. Place the chicken on the grill and grill, turning often, until the juices of the chicken run clear, 8 to 10 minutes. Divide the chicken among 6 plates and serve at once with the lime wedges.

Nutrition Info:

4 g carb, 157 cal, 5 g fat, 1 g sat fat, 63 mg chol, 0 g fib, 23 g pro, 207 mg sod • Carb Choices: 0; Exchanges: 3 lean protein

White Gazpacho

Servings: 4

Ingredients:

2 slices firm white bread, crusts removed

1⁄2 cup cold water

1 large hothouse (English) cucumber, peeled, seeded, and chopped

1 cup seedless green grapes

1⁄4 cup chopped sweet onion

1⁄4 cup slivered almonds, toasted

3 tablespoons lemon juice

1 tablespoon extra virgin olive oil

1 small garlic clove, sliced

1⁄2 teaspoon ground cumin

1⁄2 teaspoon kosher salt

Directions:

1. Place the bread and water in a shallow dish and let stand until the water is absorbed.
2. Combine the bread and all the remaining ingredients in a food processor or blender and process until smooth. Cover and refrigerate until chilled, at least 2 hours or up to 2 days. Ladle into 4 bowls and serve.

Nutrition Info:

17 g carb, 141 cal, 8 g fat, 1 g sat fat, 0 mg chol, 2 g fib, 3 g pro, 202 mg sod • Carb Choices: 1; Exchanges: 1⁄2 starch, 1⁄2 fruit, 1 fat

Wheat Berries And Vegetables with Moroccan Spices

Servings: 6

Ingredients:

2 teaspoons extra virgin olive oil

1⁄2 cup diced onion

1 garlic clove, minced

1⁄4 teaspoon ground ginger

1⁄4 teaspoon ground cumin

1⁄8 teaspoon ground cinnamon

1⁄8 teaspoon ground cayenne

1⁄4 cup Vegetable Stock or low-sodium vegetable broth

2 cups cooked wheat berries

1 small zucchini, cut into 1⁄2-inch cubes

1 small yellow squash, cut into 1⁄2-inch cubes

1⁄2 teaspoon kosher salt

2 tablespoons chopped fresh cilantro

1 teaspoon lime juice

Directions:

1. Heat a medium nonstick skillet over medium heat. Add the oil and tilt the pan to coat the bottom evenly. Add the onion and cook, stirring often, until softened, 5 minutes. Add the garlic, ginger, cumin, cinnamon, and cayenne and cook, stirring constantly, until fragrant, 30 seconds.
2. Add the stock, then add the wheat berries, zucchini, yellow squash, and salt. Cook, stirring occasionally, until the squash is crisp-tender and the liquid evaporates, about 3 minutes. Remove from the heat and stir in the cilantro and lime juice. Spoon the wheat berries into a serving dish and serve at once.

Nutrition Info:

21 g carb, 119 cal, 2 g fat, 0 g sat fat, 0 mg chol, 3 g fib, 4 g pro, 105 mg sod • Carb Choices: 1 1/2; Exchanges: 1 1/2 starch

Lemon-garlic Baked Chicken Breasts

Servings: 4

Ingredients:

4 (6-ounce) bone-in skin-on chicken breasts

1/2 teaspoon kosher salt

1/8 teaspoon freshly ground pepper

2 teaspoons extra virgin olive oil

1 cup Chicken Stock or low-sodium chicken broth

1 large lemon, thinly sliced and seeded

4 garlic cloves, crushed

2 tablespoons chopped fresh Italian parsley

Directions:

1. Preheat the oven to 375°F.
2. Gently loosen but do not detach the skin from the chicken breasts. Rub the salt and pepper over the breast underneath the skin. Heat a large ovenproof skillet over medium-high heat. Add the oil, tilt the pan to coat the bottom evenly. Place the chicken in the skillet skin side down and cook, turning once, until both sides are well browned, about 6 minutes.
3. Add the stock to the skillet. Place the lemon slices and garlic cloves around the chicken. Transfer the skillet to the oven and bake until the juices of the chicken run clear, about 30 minutes.
4. Transfer the chicken to a large plate and cover loosely with foil to keep warm. Set the skillet over medium-high heat and bring the juices to a boil. Using a fork, mash the garlic into small bits. Boil the sauce until slightly thickened, about 3 minutes. Stir in the parsley. Divide the chicken and lemon slices evenly among 4 plates. Spoon the sauce evenly over the chicken and serve at once. Remove the skin before eating.

Nutrition Info:

4 g carb, 176 cal, 5 g fat, 1 g sat fat, 72 mg chol, 1 g fib, 28 g pro, 235 mg sod • Carb Choices: 0; Exchanges: 4 lean protein, 1⁄2 fat

Pork Medallions with Fennel And Onion

Servings: 4

Ingredients:

1 medium bulb fennel

1 (1-pound) pork tenderloin, trimmed of all visible fat and cut into 12 slices

3⁄4 teaspoons kosher salt, divided

1⁄4 teaspoon freshly ground pepper, divided

4 teaspoons extra virgin olive oil, divided

1⁄2 large sweet onion, thinly sliced

2 tablespoons chopped fennel fronds or fresh Italian parsley

Directions:

1. Trim the tough outer stalks from the fennel. Cut the fennel bulb in half vertically and cut away and discard the core. Cut each half lengthwise into 1⁄4-inch slices.
2. Sprinkle the pork with 1⁄2 teaspoon of the salt and 1⁄8 teaspoon of the pepper.
3. Heat a large nonstick skillet over medium-high heat. Add 2 teaspoons of the oil and tilt the pan to coat the bottom evenly. Add the pork and cook, turning once, until well browned, about 3 minutes on each side. Transfer to a plate and cover loosely with foil to keep warm.
4. Add the remaining 2 teaspoons oil to the same skillet. Add the onion, fennel, remaining 1⁄4 teaspoon salt, and remaining 1⁄8 teaspoon pepper and cook, stirring often, until crisp-tender, about 6 minutes. Stir in the fennel fronds. Cut the tenderloin into thin slices, divide the pork and fennel mixture evenly among 4 plates, and serve at once.

Nutrition Info:

9 g carb, 210 cal, 9 g fat, 2 g sat fat, 63 mg chol, 2 g fib, 24 g pro, 290 mg sod • Carb Choices: 1⁄2; Exchanges: 2 veg, 3 lean protein, 1 fat

Sugar-and-spice Pita Chips

Servings: 8

Ingredients:

2 (6-inch) whole wheat pita breads

2 tablespoons sugar

1⁄4 teaspoon ground cinnamon

Pinch kosher salt

Directions:

1. Preheat the oven to 350°F. Line a large baking sheet with parchment paper.
2. Split each pita in half to make 4 rounds. Cut each round into 12 wedges. Place the pita wedges in a single layer on the prepared pan, rough side up.
3. Stir together the sugar, cinnamon, and salt in a small bowl. Sprinkle the pita wedges evenly with the sugar mixture.
4. Bake until the pita wedges are crisp and lightly toasted, 10 to 12 minutes. Cool the chips in the pan on a wire rack. The chips can be covered in an airtight container and stored at room temperature for up to 5 days.

Nutrition Info:

12 g carb, 55 cal, 0 g fat, 0 g sat fat, 0 mg chol, 1 g fib, 2 g pro, 94 mg sod • Carb Choices: 1; Exchanges: 1 starch

Pumpkin And Roasted Red Pepper Soup

Servings: 6

Ingredients:

2 teaspoons extra virgin olive oil

3 large carrots, peeled and chopped

1 large onion, chopped

2 garlic cloves, chopped

1⁄2 teaspoon ground cumin

1⁄2 teaspoon ground coriander

5 to 51⁄2 cups Vegetable Stock or low-sodium vegetable broth

1 large red Roasted Bell Pepper or 1 cup roasted red peppers from a jar, chopped

1⁄2 teaspoon kosher salt

1⁄4 teaspoon freshly ground pepper

1 (15-ounce) can pumpkin (not pumpkin pie filling)

2 tablespoons lemon juice

Directions:

1. Heat a large pot over medium heat. Add the oil and tilt the pan to coat the bottom evenly. Add the carrots and onion and cook, stirring often, until the vegetables are softened, 5 minutes. Add the garlic, cumin, and coriander and cook, stirring constantly, until fragrant, 30 seconds.
2. Add 5 cups of the stock, the roasted pepper, salt, and ground pepper and bring to a boil over high heat. Cover, reduce the heat to low, and simmer until the vegetables are very tender, 15 to 20 minutes.
3. Place the vegetable mixture in a food processor or blender in batches and process until smooth. Return the soup to the pot and stir in the pumpkin. Add the remaining 1⁄2 cup stock a few tablespoons at a time, if needed, to reach the desired consistency. Cook over medium heat, stirring often, until heated through. Remove from the heat and stir in the lemon juice. Ladle into 6 bowls and serve at once. The soup can be refrigerated, covered, for up to 4 days or frozen for up to 3 months.

Nutrition Info:

16 g carb, 80 cal, 2 g fat, 0 g sat fat, 0 mg chol, 4 g fib, 2 g pro, 324 mg sod • Carb Choices: 1; Exchanges: 1⁄2 starch, 2 veg

Soufflé Roll with Asparagus, Mushrooms, And Mozzarella

Servings: 12

Ingredients:

8 large eggs

4 large egg whites

1 tablespoon unsalted butter

2 tablespoons unbleached all-purpose flour

1 cup 1% low-fat milk

3⁄4 teaspoon kosher salt, divided

1⁄8 teaspoon freshly ground pepper

21⁄2 teaspoons extra virgin olive oil, divided

1 pound asparagus, tough ends removed and spears cut into 3⁄4-inch pieces

8 ounces cremini or white mushrooms, sliced

1 small onion, chopped

6 ounces shredded part-skim mozzarella (about 11⁄2 cups)

Directions:

1. Separate the eggs, placing the egg yolks in a medium bowl and the egg whites, including the 4 additional egg whites for a total of 12, in a large bowl. Set aside.
2. Melt the butter in a large saucepan over medium heat. Add the flour and whisk until smooth. Gradually whisk in the milk. Cook, whisking constantly, until the mixture comes to a boil and thickens, about 3 minutes. Whisk in 1/4 teaspoon of the salt and the pepper. Remove from the heat.
3. Whisk the egg yolks until smooth. Slowly whisk about 1/4 cup of the milk mixture into the egg yolks. Slowly whisk the egg yolk mixture into the milk mixture remaining in the saucepan. Return the mixture to medium heat and cook, whisking constantly until the mixture thickens and coats the back of a spoon. Strain through a fine wire mesh strainer into a clean bowl. Place a sheet of plastic wrap on the surface to prevent a skin from forming. Let stand to cool to room temperature.
4. Meanwhile, heat a large nonstick skillet over medium heat. Add 2 teaspoons of the oil and tilt the pan to coat the bottom evenly. Add the asparagus, mushrooms, onion, and the remaining 1/2 teaspoon salt. Cook, stirring often, until the asparagus is crisp-tender, about 6 minutes. Transfer to a bowl and set aside.
5. Preheat the oven to 400°F. Line a 15 x 10-inch jellyroll pan or large rimmed baking sheet with parchment paper and brush the paper with the remaining 1/2 teaspoon oil.
6. Beat the egg whites at high speed with an electric mixer until stiff peaks form. Fold the egg whites into the cooled milk mixture in 3 additions, stirring until no white streaks remain. Spread the batter evenly into the prepared pan. Bake until the top is lightly browned and the center is set, 12 to 15 minutes. Reduce the oven temperature to 350°F. Cool the soufflé in the pan on a wire rack for 5 minutes.
7. Turn the soufflé upside down onto a clean sheet of parchment paper. Peel off the top layer of parchment and return the parchment to the pan. Spoon the asparagus mixture evenly over the soufflé and sprinkle evenly with the mozzarella. Starting with the long end, roll the soufflé up jellyroll-style. Place the roll seam side down on the parchment paper in the baking pan. Bake until heated through, 10 to 15 minutes. Cut the roll into slices using a serrated knife. Serve hot or warm.

Nutrition Info:

5 g carb, 136 cal, 8 g fat, 4 g sat fat, 152 mg chol, 1 g fib, 10 g pro, 251 mg sod • Carb Choices: 0; Exchanges: 1 medium-fat protein, 1/2 fat

Egg And Avocado Soft Tacos

Servings: 4

Ingredients:

4 large eggs

4 large egg whites

2 tablespoons 1% low-fat milk

2 teaspoons canola oil

1⁄4 cup diced onion

1⁄4 cup diced green bell pepper

1 jalapeño, seeded and minced

1⁄2 medium avocado, pitted, peeled, and diced

4 (6-inch) whole wheat flour tortillas, warmed

1⁄2 cup salsa

Directions:

1. Combine the eggs, egg whites, and milk in a medium bowl and whisk until smooth. Set aside.
2. Heat a large nonstick skillet over medium-high heat. Add the oil and tilt the pan to coat the bottom evenly. Add the onion, bell pepper, and jalapeño and cook, stirring often, until softened, 5 minutes.
3. Add the egg mixture to the onion mixture. Cook, stirring constantly, until soft-scrambled, about 3 minutes. Stir in the avocado.
4. To assemble the tacos, spoon about 1/2 cup of the egg mixture down the center of each tortilla and top the egg mixture with 2 tablespoons of the salsa.

Nutrition Info:

27 g carb, 245 cal, 12 g fat, 2 g sat fat, 212 mg chol, 4 g fib, 14 g pro, 427 mg sod • Carb Choices: 2; Exchanges: 2 starch, 1 medium-fat protein, 1 fat

Whole Roasted Fish with Chermoula Sauce

Servings: 4

Ingredients:

2 (2-pound) dressed whole striped bass or other small whole fish

2 teaspoons ground cumin, divided

2 teaspoons paprika, divided

1 teaspoon kosher salt, divided

1⁄4 cup loosely packed fresh Italian parsley

1⁄4 cup loosely packed fresh cilantro leaves

3 tablespoons cold water

2 tablespoons extra virgin olive oil

2 tablespoons lemon juice

2 garlic cloves, coarsely chopped

Pinch of ground cayenne pepper

Directions:

1. Preheat the oven to 400°F.
2. To make the fish, cut 3 diagonal slits in each side of each of the fish. Sprinkle evenly all over with 1 teaspoon of the cumin, 1 teaspoon of the paprika, and 1⁄2 teaspoon of the salt. Place the fish in a single layer in a large baking dish. Pour just enough water into the dish to cover the bottom. Bake the fish, uncovered, until the fish flakes easily with a fork, 20 to 25 minutes.
3. Meanwhile, combine the parsley, cilantro, water, oil, lemon juice, garlic, cayenne, remaining 1 teaspoon cumin, remaining 1 teaspoon paprika, and remaining 1⁄2 teaspoon salt in a food processor and process until the mixture is finely chopped.
4. Remove the skin from the top side of each of the fish and discard. Run a knife between the flesh and bones of the top half of the fish and lift off the fillet. Turn the fish over and repeat. Divide the fish evenly among 4 plates and drizzle evenly with the sauce.

Nutrition Info:

2 g carb, 214 cal, 10 g fat, 2 g sat fat, 62 mg chol, 0 g fib, 28 g pro, 386 mg sod • Carb Choices: 0; Exchanges: 4 lean protein, 1 fat

Fish And Chips

Servings: 4

Ingredients:

Potatoes

2 medium baking potatoes (about 1 pound), well scrubbed

2 teaspoons extra virgin olive oil

1⁄4 teaspoon kosher salt

Pinch of freshly ground pepper Fish

1 teaspoon canola oil

1⁄3 cup unbleached all-purpose flour

1 large egg white

1 tablespoon water

3⁄4 cup cornflake crumbs

4 (5-ounce) thin white-fleshed fish fillets

1⁄2 teaspoon paprika

1⁄4 teaspoon kosher salt

1⁄8 teaspoon freshly ground pepper

Lemon wedges

Directions:

1. Preheat the oven to 425°F.
2. To make the potatoes, cut each potato into 8 wedges and place on a medium rimmed baking sheet. Drizzle with the oil, sprinkle with the salt and pepper, and toss to coat. Arrange the potatoes in a single layer.
3. Bake 25 minutes. Turn the wedges and bake until the potatoes are tender and well browned, 8 to 10 minutes longer.
4. Meanwhile, to make the fish, brush a medium rimmed baking sheet with the oil.
5. Place the flour in a shallow dish. Place the egg white and water in another shallow dish and beat lightly with a fork. Place the cornflake crumbs in a third shallow dish. Sprinkle the fish with the paprika, salt, and pepper. Dip the fillets, one at a time, into the flour, then into the egg white mixture, then into the cornflake crumbs, pressing to adhere. Place the fillets on the prepared baking sheet. Bake, without turning, until the crust is golden 12 to 15 minutes. Divide the fish and potatoes among 4 plates and serve at once with the lemon wedges.

Nutrition Info:

24 g carb, 259 cal, 5 g fat, 1 g sat fat, 67 mg chol, 2 g fib, 27 g pro, 450 mg sod • Carb Choices: 11⁄2; Exchanges: 11⁄2 starch, 3 lean protein, 1⁄2 fat

Hot Black Bean Dip

Servings: 33⁄4 Cups

Ingredients:

3 teaspoons canola oil, divided

1 (141⁄2-ounce) can no-salt-added diced tomatoes, undrained

2 (15-ounce) cans no-salt-added black beans, rinsed and drained, divided

1 small onion, diced

1⁄2 cup diced red bell pepper

1 jalapeño, seeded and minced

2 garlic cloves, minced

2 teaspoons chili powder

1 teaspoon ground cumin

1⁄2 teaspoon kosher salt

1⁄4 cup chopped fresh cilantro

1 tablespoon lime juice

1⁄4 cup thinly sliced scallions

2 ounces shredded reduced-fat sharp Cheddar cheese (about 1⁄2 cup)

Directions:

1. Preheat the oven to 350°F. Brush a shallow 2-quart baking dish with 1 teaspoon of the oil.
2. Place a colander inside a bowl and place the tomatoes in the colander to drain. Reserve the liquid.
3. Place 1 can of the beans in a medium bowl. Using a potato masher, mash the beans until chunky. Stir in the remaining 1 can of beans and the reserved tomato liquid. Set the bean mixture and the drained tomatoes aside.
4. Heat a large nonstick skillet over medium heat. Add the remaining 2 teaspoons oil and tilt the pan to coat the bottom evenly. Add the onion, bell pepper, and jalapeño and cook, stirring often, until the vegetables are softened, 5 minutes. Add the garlic, chili powder, cumin, and salt and cook, stirring constantly, until fragrant, 30 seconds.
5. Add the bean mixture and cook, stirring often, until heated through, about 3 minutes. Remove from the heat and stir in the cilantro and lime juice. Spoon the bean mixture into the prepared baking dish. Sprinkle with the drained tomatoes, the scallions, and Cheddar.
6. Bake, uncovered, until the dip is bubbly and the cheese melts, about 20 minutes. Serve hot or warm with fresh raw vegetables, baked tortilla chips, or baked whole wheat pita chips.

Nutrition Info:

11 g carb, 76 cal, 2 g fat, 1 g sat fat, 3 mg chol, 3 g fib, 4 g pro, 96 mg sod • Carb Choices: 1; Exchanges: 1 starch, 1 plant-based protein, 1⁄2 fat

Rice Salad with Leeks And Tomatoes

Servings: 6

Ingredients:

2 cups water

1 cup long-grain brown rice

3⁄4 teaspoon kosher salt, divided

2 medium leeks, cut in half lengthwise, sliced into 1⁄4-inch slices

2 tablespoons sherry vinegar or white wine vinegar

1 1⁄2 tablespoon extra virgin olive oil

1⁄8 teaspoon freshly ground pepper

2 cups cherry tomatoes, halved, or 1 large tomato, chopped

1 tablespoon chopped fresh thyme or 1 teaspoon dried thyme

Directions:

1. Combine the water, rice, and 1⁄2 teaspoon of the salt in a medium saucepan and bring to a boil over high heat. Reduce the heat to low, cover, and simmer until the rice is tender, 35 to 40 minutes. Drain and cool.
2. Meanwhile, submerge the sliced leeks in a large bowl of water, lift them out, and drain in a colander. Repeat, using fresh water, until no grit remains in the bottom of the bowl. In a saucepan fitted with a steamer basket, bring 1 inch of water to a boil over high heat. Add the leeks, cover, and steam until tender, about 8 minutes. Transfer to a plate to cool.
3. Whisk together the vinegar, oil, remaining 1⁄4 teaspoon salt, and the pepper in a large bowl. Add the rice, leeks, tomatoes, and thyme. Serve the salad at room temperature. The salad tastes best on the day it is made, but it can be refrigerated, covered, for up to 1 day. Let stand at room temperature 30 minutes before serving.

Nutrition Info:

30 g carb, 174 cal, 5 g fat, 1 g sat fat, 0 mg chol, 3 g fib, 4 g pro, 107 mg sod • Carb Choices: 2; Exchanges: 1 1⁄2 starch, 1 veg, 1 fat

Beef Stock

Servings: 10 Cups

Ingredients:

4 teaspoons extra virgin olive oil, divided

4 pounds meaty beef bones

12 cups cold water

2 large carrots, peeled and cut into 1-inch chunks

2 stalks celery, cut into 1-inch chunks

1 large onion, chopped

4 sprigs Italian parsley

2 garlic cloves, smashed

8 black peppercorns

2 bay leaves

1 teaspoon kosher salt

Directions:

1. Heat a large pot over medium-high heat. Add 2 teaspoons of the oil and tilt the pot to coat the bottom evenly.
2. Add half the bones and cook, turning occasionally, until well browned, about 6 minutes. Transfer to a plate. Repeat with the remaining 2 teaspoons oil and the remaining bones. Return all the bones to the pot and add the remaining ingredients.
3. Bring just to a simmer over medium heat. Reduce the heat to low and cook, partially covered, with bubbles gently coming to the surface in the center of the pot, 2 hours. Place a colander in a large bowl and pour in the stock. Discard the bones, vegetables, and seasonings. Strain the stock through a fine wire mesh strainer.
4. Let stand to cool to room temperature. Cover and refrigerate until the fat rises to the top of the stock. Remove and discard the fat. Use the stock at once or refrigerate, covered, for up to 4 days or freeze for up to 6 months.

Nutrition Info:

1 g carb, 13 cal, 0 g fat, 0 g sat fat, 3 mg chol, 0 g fib, 2 g pro, 70 mg sod • Carb Choices: 0; Exchanges: None

Balsamic-baked Sweet Onions

Servings: 4

Ingredients:

1 large sweet onion

2 teaspoons extra virgin olive oil

1⁄2 teaspoon kosher salt

1⁄8 teaspoon freshly ground pepper

3⁄4 cup balsamic vinegar

Directions:

1. Preheat the oven to 400°F.
2. Cut a thin slice off the stem and root end of the onion and discard. Peel the onion and cut into 4 slices.
3. Heat a large ovenproof skillet (large enough for the onion slices to fit in a single layer) over medium-high heat. Add the oil and tilt the pan to coat the bottom evenly. Sprinkle the onion slices with the salt and pepper and place in the skillet. Cook, carefully turning once with a wide spatula to prevent the rings from separating, until the onions are browned, about 4 minutes. Add the vinegar and bring to a boil. Transfer the skillet to the oven and bake, uncovered, turning once with a wide spatula, until the onions are tender, 40 to 45 minutes.
4. Arrange the onions on a serving platter, lifting them from the skillet with a wide spatula. Drizzle the onions with the liquid remaining in the skillet. Serve hot, warm, or at room temperature.

Nutrition Info:

13 g carb, 77 cal, 3 g fat, 0 g sat fat, 0 mg chol, 1 g fib, 1 g pro, 158 mg sod • Carb Choices: 1; Exchanges: 1 veg, 1⁄2 fat

Baked Butternut Squash Risotto

Servings: 8

Ingredients:

2 teaspoons extra virgin olive oil

1 medium onion, diced

2 garlic cloves, minced

1 cup short- or medium-grain brown rice

2 cups cubed butternut squash

1⅔ cups Vegetable Stock or low-sodium vegetable broth

1 ounce freshly grated Parmesan (about ¼ cup)

2 teaspoons chopped fresh rosemary

1 teaspoon kosher salt

⅛ teaspoon freshly ground pepper

Directions:

1. Preheat the oven to 375°F.
2. Heat a Dutch oven over medium-high heat. Add the oil and tilt the pan to coat the bottom evenly. Add the onion and cook, stirring often, until softened, 5 minutes. Add the garlic and cook, stirring constantly, until fragrant, 30 seconds.
3. Add the rice and cook, stirring constantly, 2 minutes. Add the squash and stock and bring to a boil over high heat. Cover, reduce the heat to low, and simmer 5 minutes. Remove the Dutch oven from the heat and stir in the Parmesan, rosemary, salt, and pepper. Cover and bake until the rice is tender and almost all the liquid is absorbed, 1 hour. Fluff with a fork before serving. Serve the risotto at once.

Nutrition Info:

21 g carb, 122 cal, 2 g fat, 1 g sat fat, 2 mg chol, 1 g fib, 3 g pro, 208 mg sod • Carb Choices: 1 1/2; Exchanges: 1 1/2 starch

Potato-dill-crusted Fish Fillets

Servings: 4

Ingredients:

4 1⁄2 teaspoons extra virgin olive oil, divided

2 medium Yukon Gold potatoes

2 tablespoons chopped fresh dill

4 (5-ounce) thick white-fleshed fish fillets

2 teaspoons grated lemon zest

1⁄2 teaspoon kosher salt

1⁄4 teaspoon freshly ground pepper

Directions:

1. Preheat the oven to 400°F. Brush a medium rimmed baking sheet with 1/2 teaspoon of the oil.
2. Peel the potatoes and shred them on the coarse side of a box grater. Measure 1 cup of the shredded potatoes and place them in a small bowl (discard any remaining potato). Add the dill and stir to mix well.
3. Sprinkle the fish evenly on one side with the lemon zest, salt, and pepper. Pat 1/4 cup of the potato mixture in an even layer over the seasonings on each fillet.
4. Heat a large nonstick skillet over medium heat. Add 2 teaspoons of the remaining oil and tilt the pan to coat the bottom evenly. Carefully place two of the fillets, potato side down, in the skillet. Cook until the potato is tender and browned, about 5 minutes, reducing the heat if the potato begins to brown too quickly.
5. Using a wide spatula, carefully remove the fillets from the skillet and place, potato side up, on the prepared baking sheet. Repeat with the remaining 2 teaspoons oil and remaining fish fillets.
6. Bake until the fish flakes easily with a fork, 6 to 8 minutes (carefully lift the edge of the potato on one of the fillets to test for doneness). Divide the fish among 4 plates and serve at once.

Nutrition Info:

10 g carb, 194 cal, 6 g fat, 1 g sat fat, 54 mg chol, 1 g fib, 23 g pro, 220 mg sod • Carb Choices: 1/2; Exchanges: 1/2 starch, 3 lean protein, 1 fat

Chile Pepper Meatloaf

Servings: 4

Ingredients:

2 teaspoons extra virgin olive oil

1⁄3 cup finely diced onion

1⁄3 cup finely diced red bell pepper

1 jalapeño, seeded and minced

1 garlic clove, minced

1 1⁄2 teaspoons chili powder

1 teaspoon ground cumin

1 teaspoon kosher salt

1⁄4 teaspoon freshly ground pepper

Pinch of ground cayenne

1 pound 95% lean ground beef

1⁄2 cup no-salt-added tomato sauce, divided

1⁄3 cup plain dry breadcrumbs

1⁄4 cup 1% low-fat milk

1 large egg, lightly beaten

2 tablespoons chopped fresh cilantro

Directions:

1. Preheat the oven to 350°F.
2. Heat a medium nonstick skillet over medium-high heat. Add the oil and tilt the pan to coat the bottom evenly. Add the onion, bell pepper, and jalapeño and cook, stirring often, until softened, 5 minutes. Add the garlic, chili powder, cumin, salt, ground pepper, and cayenne and cook, stirring constantly, until fragrant, 30 seconds. Transfer to a plate and let cool slightly.
3. Combine the beef, 1⁄4 cup of the tomato sauce, breadcrumbs, milk, egg, cilantro, and the onion mixture in a large bowl. Mix thoroughly with your hands. Place the mixture in a shallow baking dish and shape into an 8 x 4- inch loaf.
4. Spread the remaining 1⁄4 cup tomato sauce over the loaf and bake 1 hour. Let stand 5 minutes before slicing. Cut the meatloaf into slices, divide evenly among 4 plates, and serve at once.

Nutrition Info:

13 g carb, 251 cal, 10 g fat, 3 g sat fat, 112 mg chol, 2 g fib, 26 g pro, 449 mg sod • Carb Choices: 1; Exchanges: 1 carb, 3 lean protein, 1 fat

Alphabetical Index

CPSIA information can be obtained
at www.ICGtesting.com
Printed in the USA
BVHW090013080621
608941BV00004B/1013